God As Father

When Your Own Father Failed

VantagePoint Books

A Ministry of
THE CHRISTIAN COUNSELING AND
EDUCATIONAL FOUNDATION
Glenside, Pennsylvania

VantagePoint Books
Susan Lutz, Editor

God As Father

When Your Own Father Failed

David Powlison

3143 S. Stratford Road, Winston-Salem, NC 27103-5825
www.punchbookstore.com

Unless otherwise indicated, all Scripture quotations are from the HOLY BIBLE, NEW INTERNATIONAL VERSION®. Copyright © 1973, 1978, 1984 by International Bible Society. Used by permission of Zondervan Publishing House. All rights reserved.

Printed in the United States of America.

Library of Congress Cataloging-in-Publication Data

ISBN 0-9762308-3-6

This is love: not that we loved God, but that he loved us and sent his Son as an atoning sacrifice for our sins. (1 John 4:10)

If God is for us, who can be against us? He who did not spare his own Son, but gave him up for us all – how will he not also, along with him, graciously give us all things? (Rom. 8:31-32)

God has poured out his love into our hearts by the Holy Spirit, whom he has given us. (Rom. 5:5)

You received the Spirit of sonship. And by him we cry, "Abba! Father." The Spirit himself testifies with our spirit that we are God's children. (Rom. 8:15b-16)

How can you come to know the love of God the Father? These Scripture passages talk about two ways. First, there is an inescapable, historical fact: Jesus Christ went to an agonizing death out of love for sinners. Second, there is a powerful dynamic within our hearts: the Holy Spirit pours out God's love in us to create the child's trusting response. *Did* God act in love in history? *Does* God act now in love within our hearts? Yes! God's love is effective, both then and now.

But what about people who seem to know neither the historical fact nor the internal dynamic? The crown of thorns leaves them cold. The Holy Spirit is a theory. There is little or no "*Abba,* Father" in their hearts. How do you reach them?

How, for example, would you reach Sally? Now twenty-eight years old, Sally grew up in an abusive household. During her teen years, her father sexually molested her, putting a bitter icing on their miserable relationship. Though she became a Christian in high school, Sally felt that she could never know God as her father – her relationship with her earthly father was just too damaging. She saw God as untrustworthy, demanding, merciless and unpredictable.

How would you reach someone like Bill? His father abandoned the family when Bill was three. Now thirty-six, Bill is a mature Christian in many ways, but recently he sought counseling because of his long-standing sense that "God is remote, like my father was."

What would you say to Sally and Bill?

Two statements are often shared with people with stories like theirs. I've heard them repeatedly from Christian counselors and struggling Christians. The first says, "You can't really appreciate God as Father if you had a poor relationship with your human father." This leads to a second statement about counseling methods and Christian growth: "If you have had parent problems in your personal history, you need some sort of re-parenting or corrective emotional experience. You need the love of a father substitute, therapist, mentor, or support group before you can experience God as a loving Father."

Are these statements true? If your father was abusive, critical, neglectful or selfish, are you prevented from knowing God as a loving

2

Father? Must you first experience a corrective human relationship to make "God is my Father" a nourishing reality?

When you carefully examine these statements, they turn out to be false. They distort the nature of the human heart and why it is that people believe lies about God. Even worse, these statements deny the power and truth of God's Word and the Holy Spirit. They replace Almighty God with an almighty psychotherapist, whose tolerance and affirmations prepare the heart for a god who will merely tolerate and affirm.

This is not to say that people with poor human parents don't often project those images onto the true God. They often do, and it's no wonder that they go on to say that such a god is untrustworthy and unloving! The first statement reflects this common phenomenon: "I had a rotten parent, so I think God is rotten." But is the connection between these facts the real connection? Do people twist their view of God *because* they have had sinful parents, or for some other reason? You must dig below the surface for the answer. For example, are there any people with bad parents who have a great relationship with God? Are there any people with good parents who have a rotten view of God?

The second statement also reflects a common experience: "It really made a difference to meet a person I could trust, and my relationship with God grew." Without a doubt, good, caring, and wise friends are a tremendous help in the change process. A godly counselor is like a godly parent in many ways. But is this explanation of change, however plausible, the right one? Again, you must dig. Do affirming human relationships correct the problem of a distorted view of God, or is there a different primary solution? Are there any people who know a person they trust, yet still think God is untrustworthy? Can a relationship with a person you trust mislead you further about God?

King, Shepherd, Master, Savior, and God

Our response to these two statements should start by noting that sinful human fathers are not unique in misrepresenting God. *All* of the words God uses to describe himself have disappointing human parallels. Consider these examples:

God is King. Human rulers are frequently weak, distant, cruel or corrupt. Who is in your mind when you think about what God the King is like: Queen Elizabeth? George Bush? Saddam Hussein? The judge in traffic court? Rulers who accurately reflect God have always been rare. Yet your experience – however bad – needn't prevent you from knowing God as King and Judge. God himself tells you about good, bad, and mediocre kings so you can learn to tell the difference. The Bible also shows and tells what sort of king God is. The question is, do you allow the Word or personal experience to dictate your perception of God? If you look at God through the lens of your human experience, you do so at your peril. But to those who will listen, the Holy Spirit speaks through the Word to reinterpret our life experiences. This truth then goes on to shape our perceptions of future experience.

The LORD is my shepherd. When it comes to human shepherds, few are like Philip Keller, who portrayed so winsomely the care and wisdom of the shepherd's craft *(A Shepherd Looks at Psalm 23)*. What if the real-life shepherds you knew were ignorant laborers or drunken drifters? Or what if all you've known are storybook scenes of lambs and fair youths gamboling in green meadows? Is either picture helpful in understanding God? Does that mean that Psalm 23 is powerless to strengthen you until you know a Philip Keller-type shepherd? Of course not.

Think also about the shepherds of God's flock you've known. Some people can point with joy to a "godly pastor who made such an impact on my life." But other people grew up under false teachers – greedy, willful, and arrogant men like those in Ezekiel 34. Does this mean that you can't be comforted that the Lord is a shepherd until you know a godly pastor?

Ezekiel 34 and John 10 argue the opposite. God assumes we can hear comfort straight from him even if people have betrayed our trust: "I am against these evil shepherds, and I, the good shepherd, will myself come and take care of you, my flock." The existence of perversity does not make us blind to purity. Get first things first. The Holy Spirit often uses godly shepherds but he does not require them. He is powerful enough to reveal the Chief Shepherd even without noble human models.

"The Lord is my master, and I am his bond slave." How do people typically experience authority figures – bosses, commanding officers, CEOs, management? Often there is rivalry, estrangement, manipulation and suspicion between masters and underlings. Literal slavery has always been full of degradation and resentment. Yet God chose a word that is loaded with negative experience and expects us to experience it as a delight. He portrays himself as a kind master and us as willing slaves. What a shock Paul's slavery language must have been to resentful or despairing slaves – but how liberating, once they grasped the point! Again, God uses one-sided experience to point to two-sided truth. There are both good and bad master-slave relationships. Will you believe God or the world you've known? The Holy Spirit is able to renew our minds to trust the Lord.

"God is my Savior, Rescuer and Helper." We often have good reason to flee human beings who like to play the savior by rescuing or fixing others. They have a "messiah-complex" and are proud, meddlesome, self-righteous, and controlling. It's no fun being "helped" by such a helper! If you have only known pseudo-saviors, are you prevented from knowing Jesus Christ as your Savior? Amazingly, somehow God seems to be able to reveal himself as utterly Godly without utterly godly people showing the way.

"The LORD is God." This is the ultimate example. What is the typical human experience of "God"? Depending on who you listen to, God is a philosophical abstraction, your higher power, an idol, an experiential high during meditation, a remote tyrant, a good buddy, creative energy, a benign grandfather, or even yourself. All these images grossly misshape God. Does that mean it is impossible to know the living and true God if I

6

have spent my life hearing and worshiping such false images?

The Bible everywhere rejects such an idea and offers instead to "open their eyes and turn them from darkness to light" (Acts 26:18). God is in the business of changing people's minds; he is not hindered by distortions. He can reveal himself, shining into "our hearts to give us the light of the knowledge of the glory of God in the face of Christ" (2 Cor. 4:6). Life experience is not supreme; neither are the lies that people believe. God is, and he alone trumps what we bring to the table.

In each of these examples, it is absurd to say that life experience dictates a person's reality. On the contrary: the very experience of disappointing and distorted images can make you long to know the *real* King, Shepherd, Master, Savior and God! You might say, "My pastor never taught me about God. How I rejoice that Hebrews 13:20-21 is true, that the great Shepherd of the sheep shed his blood for me and teaches me to do his will." "My boss is manipulative and deceptive. How I rejoice that Ephesians 6:5-8 is becoming true in me and that I can serve Christ with integrity instead of being bitter or fearful!" "The God I grew up hearing about seemed like a remote killjoy. Praise the real God that Psalm 36 is true, and he is an immediate refuge and a fountain of love, light, and joy!"

Clearly, our fallen experience need not control us. Yet for many, the truth that *"God is Father"* seems to be the exception. They *do* feel that their knowledge of God the Father is controlled by the earthly parallel. So we turn to the second question: Must your own father dictate the meaning of that phrase until a substitute human father puts a new spin on it?

But Is God My Father?

Concepts from our psychologized culture saturate the way people – even Christian people – think about themselves and others. The source for the idea that your human father determines your view of the heavenly Father is psychodynamic psychology, not the Bible. It was developed by men such as Sigmund Freud and Erik Erikson, who rightly observed that people often create their own gods. Their psychodynamic theory made this "from the bottom up" pattern *the* explanation for our ideas of God. It denied that the real God revealed himself "from the top down." The psychodynamic god was a projection of the human psyche. Popular versions of this idea now permeate our culture.

"If my father didn't love me, I can't know God as a loving Father." This idea rings a bell in the human heart. But when we remember that our hearts are naturally sinful, we start to see different reasons why this explanation is so convincing to us. As sinners, we tend to manufacture false images of God, and human fathers are prime models from which to work. As sinners, we duck responsibility for our unbelief, blaming others and savoring the role of victim. As sinners, when we project lies and faulty images onto God, we may prefer to point to human fathers as the cause rather than looking to the activities of our own hearts. The psychological "insight" caters to our sinful human tendency to find excuses for our unbelief.

In an earlier generation, a common excuse for unbelief was, "The church is full of hypocrites, so I don't want anything to do with God." That was more willful and bitter: "Get lost, God." Today, the tone is more self-pitying: "I just can't seem to trust

God." But the net effect is the same. No cry of "*Abba*, Father" springs from the heart. "My father didn't love me, so my self-centeredness, self-pity, and unbelief have an underlying reason. Somebody else caused my problems; somebody else must fix them."

The therapeutic technique follows logically from these assumptions. "Your Dad was distant and mean. You think of God as distant and mean. I, your therapist, will be interested in you and nice. Knowing my love will let you think of God as like me, interested in you and nice." When stated so bluntly, that's a shocking statement. That's why it's usually insinuated, so it sneaks up on people.

The point here is important: Such "re-parenting" not only despises the Word and the Spirit; it replaces one false image of God with another. The dissatisfying god manufactured by the human soul, supposedly because of bad parents, can now be remanufactured in the image of a satisfying therapist.

It's easy to see that the living and true God is not like an abusive, rejecting, capricious parent. The real God sent Jesus Christ on a mission of love to save unacceptable people. But God is not like the benign, all-accepting therapist either. The real God has just anger and an unchanging standard, and those he loves are "helpless, ungodly, sinners, enemies" (Rom. 5). The real God is not a devil, but neither is he Carl Rogers. The "re-parenting" approach has a faulty view of who the Father is and what a parent ought to be. It knows that cruelty and neglect are wrong, but it replaces such sins with supreme confidence in the therapist's powers and affirmations of the self. There is no authoritative truth, no dying to self, and no crucified Savior in this version of love. Am I saying that caring counselors and friends are irrelevant to change? Of course not! One needn't choose between truth and love: people grow in the way Ephesians 4:15-16 describes. My point is simply that we need to get first things first so that our vision of human love connects with God's love, rather than competes with it.

People change when the Holy Spirit brings the love of God to their hearts through the gospel. Whoever receives the Spirit of adoption as God's child learns to cry out, "*Abba*, Father." People change when they see that they are responsible for what they believe about God. Life experience is no excuse for believing lies; the world and devil don't excuse the flesh. People change when biblical truth becomes more loud and vivid than previous life experience. And people change when they have ears to hear and eyes to see what God tells us about himself:

> For the LORD comforts his people and
> will have compassion on his afflicted
> ones.
> But Zion said, "The LORD has forsaken
> me, the Lord has forgotten me."
> "Can a mother forget the baby at her
> breast and have no compassion on
> the child she has borne?
> Though she may forget,
> I will not forget you!
> See, I have engraved you on the palms
> of my hands." (Isa. 49:13-16)

He does not treat us as our sins deserve
  or repay us according to our iniquities.
For as high as the heavens are above the
  earth, so great is his love for those
  who fear him;
as far as the east is from the west, so far
  has he removed our transgressions
  from us.
As a father has compassion on his children,
  so the LORD has compassion on those
  who fear him. (Ps. 103:10-13)

These things are true, both the promises and the actions that fulfill them. Through them, God addresses the fears of sufferers and sinners.

Do people come to know *this* God because human counselors skillfully re-parent them? No, and the very attempt to make that a counseling paradigm is idolatrous. But aren't good counselors like good fathers (and mothers)? Yes, of course. As the apostle Paul said:

But we were gentle among you, like a mother caring for her little children. We loved you so much that we were delighted to share with you not only the gospel of God but our lives as well, because you had become so dear to us. Surely you remember, brothers, our toil and hardship; we worked night and day in order not to be a burden to anyone while we preached the gospel of God to you.

You are witnesses, and so is God, of how holy, righteous and blameless we were among you who believed. For you know that we dealt with each of you as a father deals with his own children, encouraging, comforting and urging you to live lives worthy of God, who calls you into his kingdom and glory. (1 Thess. 2:7-12)

Why should a counselor be like this? Because God is like this. The difference between Paul's pattern and re-parenting therapy lies on the surface. Did Paul "re-parent" the Thessalonians so that, now knowing and changed by Paul's love, they would be able to envision God as loving? No, that's exactly backwards and even blasphemous.

Paul was vigorous, caring, and authoritative as a parent-counselor who carried the Father's message. The love of the Father changes people, and it changed Paul. Knowing divine love, he could then give love, a love that was the fruit and the vehicle of the message he pressed on his hearers. God is primary; the human agent is significant but secondary.

The modern re-parent/therapist reverses this. The human counselor is primary; if God is significant at all, he is only secondary. The issue at stake is not whether or not counselors should be patient, kind, and so forth. First Corinthians 13 settles that. But in God's drama of redemption, who will be the lead, and who will be the supporting actor?

If your father didn't love you, you *can* know the love of the Father. A godly counselor (or parent or friend) may be instrumental. But the key to change lies between you and God, not between you and that other person.

Getting Down to Cases

Let's look at how these truths helped Sally and Bill. As Sally acknowledged, "For years I thought I could never know God as my Father because I had such a rotten relationship with my dad. But then I realized that my biggest problem was *me*, not God or my father. My belief system was all messed up. I was projecting lies onto God and not believing what was true about him!"

Sally began to feed her faith with the truth that God the Father is faithful, merciful, and consistent. He patiently worked on her, disciplining her and teaching her to know the truth about him. Sally saw that her view of God was not *caused* by her life experience but by what her own heart had done with her experience of being wronged. As Sally repented and her mind was renewed, she was progressively freed to let go of old disappointments, bitterness, fears and demands. She became able to say wholeheartedly, "Give thanks to the LORD, for he is good, for his steadfast love endures forever."

As Bill wrestled with his sense that "God is remote, like my father was," there were three significant components to change. First, he realized that he, like all of us, tended to view his life experience as a Technicolor blockbuster, while the Bible seemed a dull, black-and-white silent movie in comparison. The flesh produces this state of affairs by interpreting life through the lens of its lies and desires. Bill began with two key truths about God as Father. First, God is abounding in mercy (Ps. 103; 2 Cor. 1:2-5). Second, God is committed to meet his children directly, to teach, to bless, and to transform (John 15:2; Heb. 12:1-14). Bill prayed and meditated these truths into his life.

13

As he learned to repent of the lies he had believed, he found the Father becoming vivid.

Second, in the process, Bill faced sins he had been avoiding. The flesh is deceitful. He found that his sentence, "God is remote, like my father was," came in part from buying into pop psychology's convenient and self-excusing diagnosis. It's true, God *did* seem distant. And Bill's father *had* been absent. But on examination the two things proved to be minimally related, much like saying, "I'm angry because I'm an Aries." Early in Bill's Christian life, God had not seemed remote at all. But some very specific patterns of sin – sexual fantasy, manipulating and avoiding people, laziness, love of money – lay beneath Bill's recurrent sense of God's distance. Psychology had turned his relationship with parents into a magic wand to explain everything that was wrong in his life. The Bible offered Bill a more concrete and life-transforming explanation.

Third, Bill found some good friends and models (Prov. 13:20; 1 Thess. 2:7-13). He had been quite isolated. He found people to know and be known by, to love and be loved by. These people did not substitute for God and re-parent Bill. They were fellow children of the Father, seeking to grow up into the Father's image. Through it all Bill began to read God into his experience – to trust and obey God – rather than continuing to read God through his life experience. No surprise, his relationship with God was transformed objectively and experientially.

Can you know God as Father even if your human father was violent, deceptive, cold...or even just occasionally disappointing? The Bible says, YES! Listen and believe, and join in fellowship with other children of the Father!

How to Get to Know Your Father

Here is a simple summary of the way to grow in the knowledge of God your Father, even if your father sinned against you.

1. Identify and take responsibility for the specific lies, false beliefs, desires, expectations and fears that poison your relationship with God.

2. Find and apply specific truths in the Bible that contend with those lies and cravings. There ought to be a battle going on within you daily as God's light and love battle your darkness.

3. Turn to God for mercy and help, so that the Spirit of truth would renew you, pouring out his love freely.

4. Take responsibility for the particular sins you express towards your father and, as generalized patterns, towards other people: bitterness, willfulness, avoidance, blame-shifting, brooding, fears, people-pleasing, slander, lying, self-pity, etc.

5. Turn to God for mercy and help, that the Spirit of love would enable you to bear his fruit thankfully.

6. Identify the specific sins committed against you. Fathers who are selfish or hostile, who lie or betray trust, who duck responsibility, are fathers who do evil. The love of God gives you courage to look evil in the eye. Identifying wrong helps you know what to forgive. It also makes clear what God calls you to tackle constructively. You need humility to recognize that some wrongs may be perceived wrongs – products of your own expectations – not real wrongs. Repenting of your own sins clears your mind to sort out evil done from evil merely perceived. You also need a renewed mind to understand that some things you were told or you

assumed were right may actually be wrong.

7. Ponder the good things your father did for you. Often bitterness and disappointment cloud the love that was shown. There are some fathers who seem to incarnate evil, but most are a mix of love and selfishness.

8. The Father gives us power to return good for evil rather than evil for evil. He remakes his children like his Son, Jesus. Come up with a plan for specific changes in how you deal with your father and his wrongs: forgiving, giving love, seeking forgiveness, forbearing, confronting constructively, refocusing your attention, pouring your energies into God's calling, etc.

9. Find wise believers to pray for you, hold you accountable, encourage, and counsel you. Faith in God our Father is catching. Wisdom for living as a peacemaker and a son of God is also catching. "The companion of the wise becomes wise."

The Father is seeking worshipers and creating children who know him. So ask, seek, and knock, and come to know him as he is.

David Powlison, M.Div., Ph.D., edits *The Journal of Biblical Counseling,* counsels and teaches in the Christian Counseling and Educational Foundation's School of Biblical Counseling, and teaches Practical Theology at Westminster Theological Seminary. He has written *Power Encounters: Reclaiming Spiritual Warfare; Competent to Counsel?: The History of a Conservative Protestant Anti-Psychiatry Movement; Seeing with New Eyes: Counseling and the Human Condition Through the Lens of Scripture* and numerous articles on counseling. David and his wife, Nan, have a son and two daughters.

Other Booklets by Our Authors

A.D.D.: Wandering Minds and Wired Bodies, by Edward T. Welch

Anger: Escaping the Maze, by David Powlison

Angry at God?: Bring Him Your Doubts and Questions, by Robert D. Jones

Bad Memories: Getting Past Your Past, by Robert D. Jones

Depression: The Way Up When You Are Down, by Edward T. Welch

Domestic Abuse: How to Help, by David Powlison, Paul David Tripp, and Edward T. Welch

Forgiveness: "I Just Can't Forgive Myself!" by Robert D. Jones

Forgiving Others: Joining Wisdom and Love, by Timothy S. Lane

God's Love: Better than Unconditional, by David Powlison

Grief: Finding Hope Again, by Paul David Tripp

Guidance: Have I Missed God's Best? By James C. Petty

Homosexuality: Speaking the Truth in Love, by Edward T. Welch

"Just One More": When Desires Don't Take No for an Answer, by Edward T. Welch

Marriage: Whose Dream? by Paul David Tripp

Motives: "Why Do I Do the Things I Do?" by Edward T. Welch

OCD: Freedom for the Obsessive-Compulsive, Michael R. Emlet

Pornography: Slaying the Dragon, by David Powlison

Pre-Engagement: 5 Questions to Ask Yourselves,
   by David Powlison and John Yenchko
Priorities: Mastering Time Management, by James
   C. Petty
Procrastination: First Steps to Change, by Walter
   Henegar
Self-Injury: When Pain Feels Good, by Edward T.
   Welch
*Sexual Sin: Combating the Drifting and
   Cheating,* by Jeffrey S. Black
Stress: Peace Amid Pressure by David Powlison
Suffering: Eternity Makes a Difference, by Paul
   David Tripp
Suicide: Understanding and Intervening by
   Jeffrey S. Black
Teens and Sex: How Should We Teach Them? by
   Paul David Tripp
Thankfulness: Even When It Hurts, by Susan Lutz
Why Me? Comfort for the Victimized by David
   Powlison
Worry: Pursuing a Better Path to Peace, by David
   Powlison

These booklets, as well as video tapes, DVDs,
CDs and audio cassettes by our authors, may be
ordered through www.ccef.org.
Speaking engagements with the authors may be
requested by visiting the Christian Counseling and
Educational Foundation website: www.ccef.org.